Written by **Tony Lynch**
Edited by **Melanie J Clayden**
Design by **Louise Ivimy** and **Susan Bartram**

Published by
Grandreams Limited
Jadwin House
205-211 Kentish Town Road
London NW5 2JU

The condensed story in this annual is adapted from the original *Jurassic Park* script.

Printed in Italy

CONTENTS

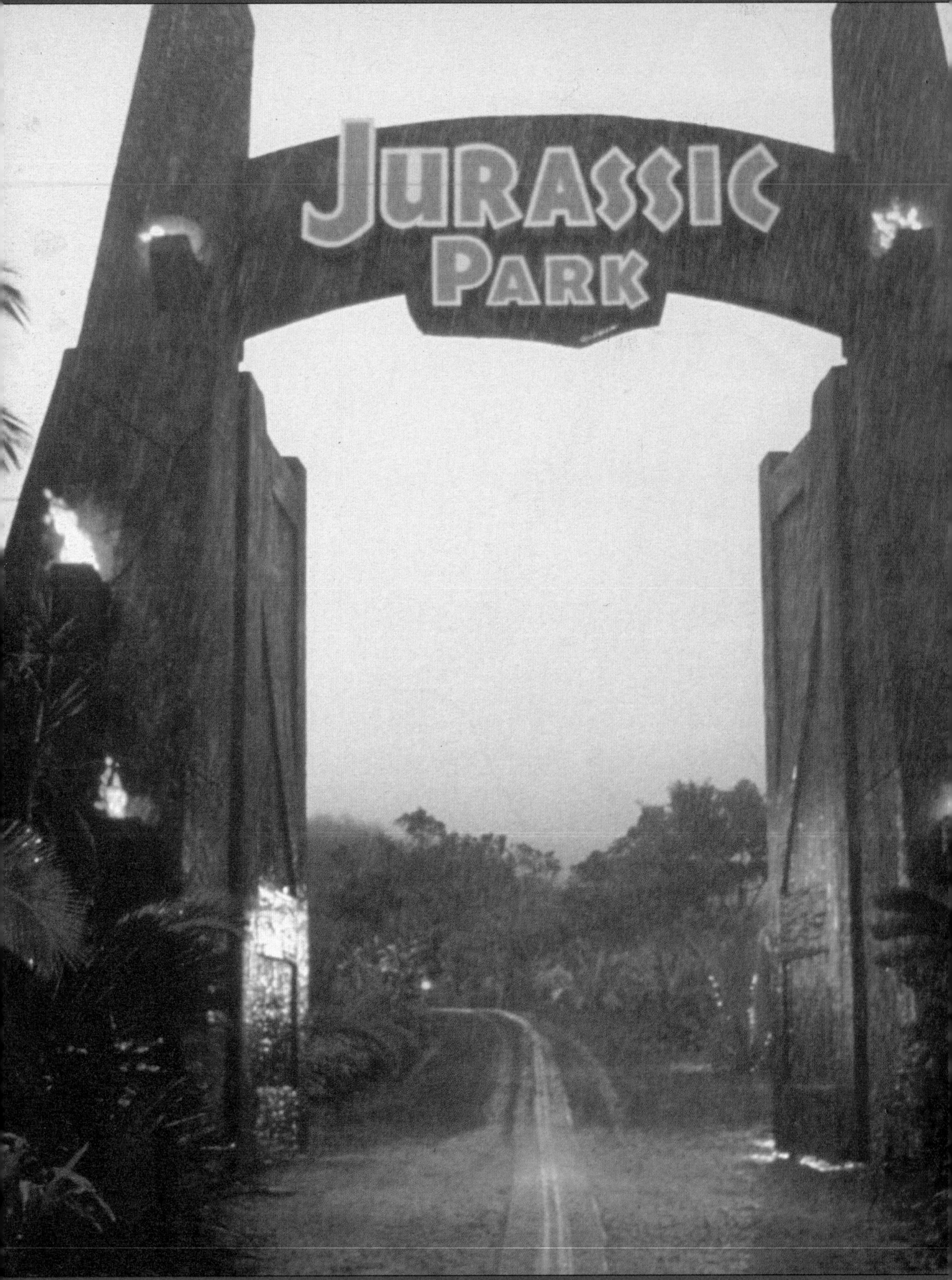
JURASSIC
PARK

WELCOME TO JURASSIC PARK.....

"This is not science fiction; it's science eventuality."
(Steven Spielberg)

Steven Spielberg's *Jurassic Park* is the movie sensation of the '90's.

Featuring some of the finest special effects in the history of cinema, *Jurassic Park* has thrilled audiences worldwide with its superb recreation of the age of the dinosaurs.

Based on the worldwide best selling novel by Michael Crichton, the film recounts the effects of man's meddling with the forces of nature for his own gain and profit.

As the author has said: "You decide you'll control nature, and from that moment on, you're in deep trouble because you can't do it. You can make a boat, but you can't make the ocean. You can make an airplane, but you can't make the air. Your powers are much less than your dreams of reason would have you believe."

This book includes the dramatic story of *Jurassic Park*...profiles director Steven Spielberg and his superstar cast...and takes an in-depth look at the fearsome dinosaurs featured in the film.

Beyond these gates lies Jurassic Park, the most amazing theme park on earth.
A kind of safari park of the past.
It's every child's dream.
It's also a potential nightmare...

THE STORY

It began way back in the mists of time, millions of years ago, when dinosaurs roamed the earth.

Fearsome looking creatures - Tyrannosaurus Rex, Dilophosaurus, Brachiosaurus, Gallimimus, Triceratops, the vicious Velociraptor and many others - ruled the world in the days before man. The carnivores stalked and killed other animals, while the herbivores fed on the leaves of trees and bushes.

As the dinosaurs ate, mosquitos sucked their blood. Many of these insects were trapped in amber - fossilised tree sap - a beautiful yellow resin which preserves forever anything that happens to get caught in it.

Preserved within the long dead mosquito was the DNA of the dinosaur.

John Hammond, a billionaire entrepreneur of vision, charm and ruthless determination, has masterminded a vast project, researching the possibilities of cloning prehistoric DNA.

His giant In-Gen Corporation mines the amber and extracts the dinosaur DNA. Then his scientists complete the genetic code by filling any 'gaps' with the DNA of frogs. It is then inserted into ostrich or emu eggs - when they hatch, the dinosaur lives again.

The animals are kept in a purpose built nature preserve called Jurassic Park on Isla Nublar, off the Costa Rican coast...

When a worker loses a leg during the transportation of a vicious Velociraptor in Jurassic Park, his family plans to sue the In-Gen Corporation for $20 million. This prompts the company's insurers to order a thorough investigation of the entire project.

Hammond invites prominent paleontologist Dr Alan Grant and paleobotanist Dr Ellie Sattler to look over Jurassic Park. "I need your endorsement," he tells them.

They are reluctant to leave their dinosaur dig in Montana, but Hammond persuades them by promising to fully fund their project for three years.

Grant, Sattler and Hammond complete the last leg of their journey to Isla Nublar in an In-Gen Corporation helicopter. Also on board is In-Gen's lawyer, Donald Gennaro, and mathematician, Dr Ian Malcolm, who is involved in the investigation.

Suddenly, the helicopter plummets dramatically and cliff walls race past the windows. "Bad wind shears," explains Hammond. "We'll have to drop pretty fast."

Then the helicopter rises again, caught on a sudden updraft, before finally bumping down on the landing pod.

"Welcome to Jurassic Park," says Hammond.

The group are driven, in two Jeeps, through huge gates in a 30 foot electrified fence. Gennaro asks Hammond if the fifty miles of perimeter fences are in place.

"Yes, and the moats, and the motion sensor tracking system," Hammond assures him.

"This is a serious investigation of the stability of the island," Gennaro warns. "If those experts aren't convinced, *I'm* not convinced. And *I* can shut you down."

In the other Jeep, Sattler is fascinated by the island's unusual plant life. She grabs a leaf as they pass by. "This shouldn't be here..."

Grant is staring at the tree trunks - some of them are grey. He looks higher and higher until he realises it is not a tree trunk at all, but the leg of a dinosaur!

It is a Brachiosaurus, chewing on the branches of a tree 35 feet above them.

From the edge of the moat, Grant and Sattler look out at hundreds of other dinosaurs on the plain below. "Look at the way they're herding," says Grant. "They *do* move in herds."

"We were right," says Sattler.

"I needed you to be right," says Hammond. "We designed this place with *your* work on habit restrictions in mind..."

In the lobby of the Visitors' Centre, the party is greeted by the sight of two enormous skeletons - a Tyrannosaur 'attacking' a Sauropod.

They are shown the audio-visual presentation which has been prepared for future visitors to the Park. Using a cartoon character called 'Mr DNA', the presentation explains how the dinosaurs have been recreated by the cloning of DNA preserved inside mosquitos in amber.

In the Fertilisation Lab, they watch the hatching of a Velociraptor. Hammond proudly tells them that he has been present at the birth of every animal on the island.

"Surely not the ones bred in the wild?" asks Malcolm.

A lab technician, Henry Wu, assures Malcolm that no dinosaurs have been born outside the laboratory. "Population control is one of our security precautions..."

"How do you know they can't breed?" Malcolm persists.

"Because all the animals in Jurassic Park are females," explains Wu. "We control their chromosomes."

Malcolm is convinced that such rigid control is impossible. "If there's one thing that evolution has taught us, it's that life will not be contained. Life breaks free...it crashes through barriers."

"You're implying a group of female animals will breed?"

"I'm simply saying that life...finds a way," says Malcolm.

The guests watch a crane lowering a steer into the foliage in the Velociraptor pen. Suddenly the plants sway and snap. The crane jerks like a fishing rod getting a bite - and a wet, crunching sound is heard as the steer is torn to pieces.

"Fast animals, aren't they?" says Hammond.

Grant questions Robert Muldoon, the Park's game warden, about the Raptors. "What metabolism do they have? What's their growth rate?"

"They're lethal at eight months," says Muldoon. "And I do mean lethal. I've hunted everything that can hunt you, but the way these things move..."

"Fast for bipeds?"

"Cheetah speed - 50-60 mph - if they ever got in the open. They're astonishing jumpers...and they show intelligence..."

The crane whirrs and the end of the cable comes into view. The steer has gone. Only the tattered, blood-stained harness remains.

"Who's hungry?" asks Hammond.

John Hammond leads his guests under the dinosaur skeletons in the lobby

During lunch, Hammond shows more of his presentation, describing planned future attractions. "We've spared no expense," he says.

"And we can charge anything we want," says Gennaro, as a recorded commentary confirms that, '...combined revenue should reach eight to nine billion dollars a year...'

"That's conservative, of course," says Hammond.

Malcolm is disgusted by the tone of the conversation. "The lack of humility before nature staggers me."

"Thank you, Dr Malcolm, but I think things are a little different than you and I had feared," Gennaro replies.

"Yes, they are. They're far worse. Genetic power is the most awesome force the planet has ever seen. The problem with the scientific power you've used is that it required no discipline to attain it. You took no responsibility for it. You simply stood on the shoulders of geniuses to accomplish something as fast as you could. And before you even knew what you had, you patented it, packaged it, slapped it on a plastic lunchbox and sold it."

"You don't give us our due credit," responds Hammond. "Our scientists have done things no-one could ever do before...Why not give an extinct species a second chance?"

"Hold on. This is no species obliterated by deforestation or the building of a dam," argues Malcolm. "Dinosaurs had their shot. Nature *selected* them for extinction."

Grant reserves judgement. "I

Tim and Lex are greeted by their grandfather

feel elated...and frightened," he says. "The world has just changed so radically, we're all running to catch up. Dinosaurs and man - two species separated by 65 million years - suddenly thrown back in the mix together. How can we know what to expect?"

The discussion is interrupted by the arrival of Hammond's grandchildren - Lex, and her younger brother, Tim.

"They're coming with us?" exclaims the incredulous Grant.

Computer screens in the control room

Hammond leads Sattler to one of the computer-guided Jeep Explorers

Grant, Sattler, Malcolm, Gennaro and the children climb aboard two computer-guided Jeep Explorers, in which they are to take the automated tour of the Park. They are monitored from the control room by Hammond, his chief technician, Ray Arnold, his computer expert, Dennis Nedry, and Game Warden, Muldoon.

The tour pauses on top of a low rise, and the recorded commentary in the Explorers tells the guests they should be seeing a Dilophosaur herd. But there is nothing to be seen and everyone is disappointed.

Meanwhile, Ray Arnold is complaining to Dennis Nedry about the tour vehicle headlights. "...they don't respond. They shouldn't be running off the car batteries. We've got all the problems of a major theme park and a major zoo and the computer's not even on its feet yet."

Nedry is glued to a TV game show. Hammond turns to him, "Dennis, our lives are in your hands, and you've got butterfingers."

"I am totally unappreciated in my time," replies the big man. "We can run the whole Park from this room, with minimal staff, for up to three days. You think that kind of automation is easy? Or cheap?"

"I'm sorry about your financial problems," says Hammond. "But they are *your* problems."

Unknown to Hammond, or anyone else in Jurassic Park, Nedry's money worries have already driven him to accept a huge bribe from one of In-Gen's biggest rivals, to steal a number of dinosaur embryos. He plans to smuggle them aboard a ship at Isla Nublar's East Dock.

"Dennis - the headlights," says Arnold.

"I'll de-bug the program when they get back," says Nedry. "It'll eat a lot of computer cycles. Parts of the system may go down for a while..."

"Quiet," says Muldoon. "They're coming to the Tyrannosaur paddock..."

Beyond a fifteen foot fence hung with 'Danger' signs, a cage rises automatically from underground. Everyone presses against the windows of the Explorers, as the bars of the cage retract - leaving a goat tethered to a stake.

"What's going to happen to the goat?" asks Lex, a look of horror suddenly crossing her face. "It's going to eat the goat!"

"Excellent!" says Tim.

"What's the matter...you never had lamb chops?" says Gennaro.

Nothing happens.

Malcolm speaks into the microphones: "You do plan to have dinosaurs on your dinosaur tour, right?"

"I really hate that guy," says Hammond in the control room.

Frustrated at not seeing a single dinosaur, the members of the tour party leave the Jeeps - much to the astonishment of the controllers - but suddenly stop in their tracks at the sight of a Triceratops laying on its side. The animal has been tranquilised and is being tended to by Gerry Harding, a veterinarian.

"An actual living, breathing Triceratops," says Sattler, in wonder.

After a long examination of the beast - and with Tim's help - Dr Sattler diagnoses that the Triceratops makes itself sick by swallowing poison berries.

A tropical storm is brewing and Gennaro insists they all return to the Explorers. But Sattler decides to stay with the vet and the sick Triceratops.

Tim looks on as Sattler and Grant examine the sick Triceratops. "This guy used to be my No.1 favourite when I was a kid," says Grant. "Still is."

Because of the impending storm, Hammond reluctantly orders the cancellation of the tour, and Arnold re-routes the program.

Meanwhile, Nedry surreptitiously phones the Mate on board the ship at the East Dock. "... Just give me fifteen minutes," he whispers. "I'll be there in ten."

He leaves the control room, nervously delivering a well-rehearsed 'after thought' as he goes. "I've finished de-bugging the phones, but the system's compiling for eighteen minutes. One or two minor circuits may switch off."

Turning to his screen he selects the 'Execute' option while starting a digital stopwatch in his hand.

Nedry's plan is now under way. The door of the Fertilisation Lab unlocks right on cue. He goes into the Cooler, taking a shaving cream can from his pocket. He flips open the bottom of the can to reveal a cooled compartment inside.

One by one, he removes dozens of glass slides - each labelled with a different dinosaur species - and slips them into the can.

"That's odd," says Arnold, in the control room. "A door system is shutting down."

"Well, Nedry said a few systems would go off line, didn't he?" replies Hammond.

"What the hell?" says Arnold. "Now fences are failing all over the Park."

"Find Nedry," commands Hammond, as all the moniters go down with a faint electronic zip. "Get it all back on. Use Nedry's terminal. He can de-bug later."

With the power off, Nedry has been able to enter the Park. He is driving a Jeep through the pouring rain. But he can barely see ahead, and the Jeep crashes into a signpost. He gets out, picks up the sign - which reads 'To the Docks' - then consults a map before driving off again.

In the Tyrannosaur paddock, the goat still bleats in the rain while the Explorers remain by the fence.

Tim has discovered a pair of heavy-duty goggles beneath the passenger seat. He puts them on and sees the florescent green image of the other Explorer. "Wow! Night vision!"

Then he feels the Jeep vibrating. Gennaro's eyes snap open as he feels it too. "M-Maybe it's the power trying to come back on," he says, nervously.

Through the goggles, Tim sees that the goat has gone - only the chain remains.

Then a dismembered goat leg crashes onto the roof of the Explorer!

Tim peels off the goggles and presses his face against the window, looking up until, through the plexibubble sun roof, he sees a *Tyrannosaurus Rex* - at least 40 feet long and 25 feet high. It swallows the goat in one gulp.

Terrified, Gennaro shoves the door open and runs toward a cement block building about 30 yards away. "He left us...He left us alone," screams Lex.

From the second Explorer, Malcolm watches the posts collapsing and the wires snapping free as the Rex chews its way through the fence.

"Don't move," whispers Grant. "Its visual acuity is based on movement."

Malcolm freezes as the beast peers in at his window, its yellow eye almost as big as the entire pane of glass.

In the first Explorer, Lex scrambles around for anything that might help. She

Lex wishes she hadn't switched on the flashlight!

finds a flashlight...she switches it on.

"Lex, don't!" yells Tim. But the beam has already attracted the Rex.

"I'm sorry...I'm sorry," squeals Lex, as she kills the light.

"Shhhhhhhhh..."

The Rex bends - and for a moment is eye-to-eye with Tim. It raises its head, peers in at the children through the sun roof and lets out a roar that rattles the windows.

Tim and Lex are trapped beneath the plexibubble which comes loose as the Rex smashes down on it. It holds, protecting them for a moment, until cracks race across it. Tim pushes back with both feet - there is only an inch of glass between him and the huge teeth.

Grant and Malcolm watch in horror as the Rex claws at the other car, the windows breaking as it rolls onto its side. The Rex shoves the car towards the broken barrier and, beyond it, a precipice above a sixty foot drop.

The car flips onto its roof and the Rex tears at the undercarriage, ripping off the rear axle. A tyre explodes, startling the animal for a moment. Then there's a loud crunch and Tim is pinned beneath a seat.

Fearful that the Rex is about to fling the car over the precipice, Grant grabs a flare and jumps out of the second Explorer. "Hey! Over here! Hey!" he yells, tossing the flare over the edge.

The Rex is about to lunge at the flame. But, instead, it whirls around and chases Malcolm who is attempting to escape. It catches him near the building and flicks him into the air with its snout. He sails right through a wooden partition and the huge head crashes through the wall after him.

The Rex sees Gennaro cowering in a corner, covering his head with his hands. The beast lunges. Gennaro emits a piercing scream - then everything falls silent.

Grant scrambles across to the upturned Explorer and pulls Lex out. "Your brother?"

"He's knocked out."

"Are you okay?"

She doesn't answer, but screams as she sees the Rex moving towards them again.

"Shhh," says Grant. "He can't see us if we don't move."

The Rex swoops to sniff at the Explorer, bits of ragged flesh and clothing hang from its mouth. The nose snorts, blowing Grant's hat from his head. He and Lex remain frozen to the spot.

Then the car is spun around and they are forced to scramble

The Rex would rather taste Tim - than a tyre!

ahead of it on hands and knees. They are trapped between the car and the sheer drop.

Tim comes round and attempts to untangle himself as the Rex stretches its huge tongue into the car, searching for him. He screams, kicking at the tongue which eventually withdraws. The Rex roars in frustration.

Grant grabs Lex and swings her onto his back. She clings onto his neck as he scrambles to the edge of the precipice. He grabs a dangling cable, slick with rain, and hanging on for dear life, they slide down. The Explorer teeters on the edge, threatening to fall on them.

The car groans. Grant attempts to swing across to another cable to take them out of the line of danger. He falls short on the first swing, but the momentum carries them back and he grabs the other cable - just as the car falls. Lex screams as the Explorer crunches upside down into the top of the tree 15 feet below them.

The Rex stares down, roars again, then withdraws.

"I will kill Nedry...I will kill him," yells Hammond, in the control room.

"There's no sign of him," says Muldoon.

Arnold stares at the mass of commands on Nedry's screen.

"Are you *doing* something?" asks Dr Sattler.

Arnold explains that he is searching the lines of code one by one, trying to discover what Nedry has done to the system.

"How many lines of code are there?" asks Sattler.

"About two million."

"I can't get Jurassic Park back on line without Dennis Nedry," says Hammond.

Nedry, glancing down at the stopwatch,

The Dilophosaurus prepares to spit a glob of poisonous goo right into Nedry's face!

while driving as fast as he can, doesn't see a cement wall straight ahead - until it's too late. He stands on the brakes but the Jeep slides out of control and onto a muddy embankment. He drops the car into reverse, but the wheels spin and dig in further.

Shoving the shaving cream can into his pocket, he picks up a flashlight and gets out. He uncranks a winch at the front of the Jeep and begins to carry the wire towards a tree across the road. "...tie it to a thing...pull it down the thing..." he mutters.

He hears a soft hooting sound, flashes the light around, but sees nothing. Checking the stopwatch, he resumes his work. "Two minutes...no problem."

Then he freezes, seeing a Dilophosaurus in the distance - spotted like an owl, with a brilliantly coloured crest behind its head. It hardly looks dangerous.

As Nedry starts back across the road, he shoos the Dilophosaurus away. But it hops along beside him, then circles him, hooting.

"Go on! Go on! Dinner time," says Nedry. "Are you hungry? Then I'll feed you." But the animal just tilts its head curiously. Nedry picks up a stick and throws it. "Fetch!"

The Dilophosaurus ducks behind a tree and pops out on the other side, hooting. "What's the matter with you," says Nedry. "Walnut brain. Extinct kangeroo. Hope I run over you."

Suddenly, the Dilophosaurus hops out right in front of him and he falls back on the seat of his pants. He scrambles to his feet, picks up a rock and throws it at the animal. "I said...beat it."

The dinosaur hops away as Nedry begins to winch his Jeep out of the mud. He looks up. The animal is about 20 feet away and staring at him. Its head goes back, then snaps forward.

"What are you do..." says Nedry, as a glob of something wet hits him in the

but manages to feel his way inside as the Dilophosaurus hoots again - from inside the Jeep!

The dinosaur is right there beside him on the passenger's seat, its crest vibrating angrily. Then it pounces, slamming him against the window. The shaving cream flies out of Nedry's pocket and by the time he has stopped screaming it is already lost in the mud.

The rain has almost stopped. Lex sobs as Grant washes blood from his face in a puddle. He pats her head, awkwardly, "Hey, come on. Don't...don't..." She flings her arms around his waist and clings to him.

There is a cracking sound as the Explorer falls a few feet further in the tree. Grant tries to prise her hands free, but she cries again. "Shhh. I'm right here, Lex."

The angry Dilophosaurus

She still clings on as he takes her towards a large culvert protruding from the barrier wall. "I have to help your brother...I want you to sit here and wait for me."

Lex eventually releases her grip and scampers into the culvert.

The Explorer is wedged in the tree. Grant climbs up and opens the driver's door to see Tim huddled on the other side.

chest. He tries to wipe away the goo that dribbles down his jacket.

Another glob hits a headlight as the confused Nedry flexes the hand which had touched the spit. The Dilophosaurus is hissing and two bulbous sacs swell on either side of its neck. The crest flares wildly. The head rears again and spits another glob - right into Nedry's face.

He screams in agony, frantically trying to rub away the venom. He flails his arms and claws at his eyes, unable to see. He smashes his head on the door of the Jeep,

"I threw up," says Tim.

"That's okay," says Grant, "I won't tell anyone. Just give me your hand." But they are still a foot apart and, as he reaches for the boy, the Explorer rocks and groans, and lurches lower in the tree.

"Go Tim...Go!" yells Grant.

Almost falling, they climb down as fast as they can - with the car smashing its way through above them. There is no escape. Miraculously, they are unhurt as the car lands upside down over them.

"I hate cars," says Grant.

Sattler and Muldoon get out of a Jeep near the wrecked building. The game warden investigates the rubble, while, 20 yards away, Sattler looks over the second Explorer.

"Did you find any..?" calls Sattler. "...Aw God!"

"I think this was Gennaro," says Muldoon, looking at something on the ground.

"I think *this* was too."

The Rex roars from somewhere in the distance. "It could be anywhere," says Muldoon.

They hear a moaning from the rubble and discover the semi-conscious Malcolm there, his face streaked with blood and his ankle twisted at a strange angle. "Any chance of moving him?" asks Sattler.

"Please," groans Malcolm." Chance it."

They lay him in the back of the Jeep and leave him there while they continue to search for Grant and the children. Malcolm looks down at a puddle in which the water is vibrating. He hears a booming noise, getting closer. Finding nothing, Sattler and Muldoon return to the Jeep. "Listen!" says Malcolm.

The booming is much louder now, and faster. Sattler looks around and sees the Rex smashing its way out of the foliage behind them.

"Go! Go! Go!" screams Malcolm, as Muldoon guns the engine. But the Jeep is slow in working through the low gears and the Rex is gaining on them. A branch shatters the wind shield, but they drive on, picking up speed. The Rex lunges at the Jeep and crunches into the left rear side. Malcolm is thrown forward, and knocks the gear shift into neutral. The engine races helplessly, until Muldoon manages to re-engage it. Then the Jeep races on and the Rex gives up the chase.

"Think they'll have *that* on the tour?" says Malcolm.

"Hey! We're here!" yells Tim, waving his arms at a motion sensor.

"Won't work," says Grant. "If the power's off, so are the sensors."

They march on, trying to find the

In the morning they wake to see a Brachiosaurus feeding on the leaves right next to them

Visitors' Centre, as night begins to fall. Suddenly, Grant hears the sound of a distant roar - but tries not to show it.

"What was that?" asks Lex.

"I didn't hear anything," says Grant, scanning the trees for somewhere to hide. "We should find someplace to rest..." The roar sounds again. "...Now!" They run to the trees and start climbing.

High up, they sit with their feet dangling over the jungle. Spread before them is a beautiful moonlit view dominated by many Sauropod heads on long necks, towering over Jurassic Park.

"Brontosaurus," says Tim. "I mean Brachiosaurus."

"It's okay to call them Brontosaurus," says Grant. "It's a great name...means 'Thunder Lizard'."

They settle in for the night, listening to the sounds of the dinosaurs. "They're singing," says Grant, a look of confusion crossing his face. "That's odd..."

"What?" asks Tim.

"Well, no-one's ever heard one before - but that sounds suspiciously like a mating call...But in an all-female environment?"

Grant hoots, trying to imitate the

call. Immediately, five or six heads turn and hoot back.

"Don't do that again," pleads Lex. "Don't get the monsters over here."

"They're not monsters, just animals - and they're herbivores," says Grant.

"They only eat vegetation," explains Tim.

"Well, I don't like the *other* kind," says Lex.

Grant awakens next morning with both children cradled in his arms. He sees the enormous head of a dinsoaur pushing into the branches beside him. The children awaken with a start. Tim just points, his mouth wide open. Lex tries to speak, but no words will come.

"It's okay," says Grant. "It's a Brachiosaurus."

"Veggisaurus, Lex, *veggi*," says Tim, scampering onto a higher branch and reaching down to pet the head. Grant moves in closer and pulls down the animal's lip to observe the jaws at work. The Brachiosaurus keeps on chewing and doesn't seem to mind the inspection at all.

"Come on, Lex. Just think of it as a big cow," says Grant.

She edges nervously forward. But the Brachiosaurus sneezes - a vast explosion right at her. "Eeeeewwww!" she cries.

Then the dinosaur hears a call from the park and walks away.

They climb down and Lex stomps off, embarrassed. "Great," says Tim. "Now she'll never try anything...just sit in her room and play with her computer."

"I'm a hacker!"

"That's what I said, nerd."

"Oh my..." says Grant, staring at something in his hand. He holds up a thin white fragment.

"What is it?" asks Tim.

"A dinosaur egg...The dinosaurs are breeding."

"But Grandpa said all the dinosaurs were girls."

"They used frog DNA to fill the gene sequence gaps," explains Grant. "And some West African frogs have been known to change sex in a single-sex environment. Malcolm was right...life found a way!"

Hammond decides to take a calculated risk, by shutting down the computer system to wipe out all of Nedry's commands. "If I understand it correctly, all the systems should come back on again in their original start-up modes - yes?"

"Theoretically," says Arnold. "But we've *never* shut down the *whole* system. It may not come back on at all."

"We could get the phones back on," says Dr Sattler.

"People are dying. Just shut down the system," commands Hammond.

Grant and the children are about a mile from the Visitors' Centre, when they see a stampede of Gallimimus in the distance.

"Look at the wheeling," says Grant. "The uniform direction change. Like a flock

Grant leads Tim and Lex through the Park

of birds evading a predator."

Suddenly, the roar of the Rex is all around them. The stampeding herd changes direction again - and heads straight for Grant and the children.

Knowing they can't make it to the trees, Grant shoves Lex and Tim under a large root system, then follows them inside. They cover their heads, bits of earth and wood fly everywhere as the herd thunders over the roots.

Eventually, the stampede passes and Grant looks out to see the herd running along the jungle's edge. The Rex suddenly roars out of the trees, cuts off the herd, runs down a single Gallimimus and makes the kill in a cloud of dust.

Some of the systems have come back on line, others haven't. Arnold reckons the shutdown has triggered some circuit breakers out in the maintenance shed at the other end of the compound, and he's gone to re-set them.

But that was a while ago and Dr Sattler is getting anxious. "I can't wait anymore," she says. "*I'm* going to get the power back on."

"I'll ride shot gun," offers Muldoon, removing a rifle from a steel cabinet.

Hammond and Malcolm spread a blueprint on a crate, while Sattler finds a walkie-talkie and flashlight with a battery-belt.

"Think you can follow those and talk us through?" asks Sattler.

"Absolutely," replies Hammond. "Just...be careful."

Grant and the children have reached the fence. Grant pokes the wire with a stick. No sparks fly. He pokes it again, with his finger. Nothing happens. "Power's still off. It's a pretty big climb though. You guys think you can make it?"

"Nope," says Tim.

"Way too high," says Lex.

Then the Rex roars in the distance, and both children leap to their feet.

"Keep moving," says Muldoon, as he and Sattler emerge into an open space near the Raptor pen. But they both freeze when they see a twisted, gnawed hole in the fence.

"The shutdown turned off all the fences," says Muldoon.

"I can see the shed from here," says Sattler. "We can make it if we run."

"No, we can't..."

"Why?"

"Because we're being hunted. From the bushes to your left..."

Dr Sattler turns to see a shadow moving in the foliage.

"It's alright," says Muldoon, raising the rifle. "I've got her."

Sattler backs slowly down the path towards the shed, then breaks into a run. She finally makes it, slamming the door behind her.

As Grant, Tim and Lex climb the fence, Malcolm and Hammond hover over the complex plan of the maintenance shed. Hammond grips the walkie-talkie, which suddenly crackles into life.

Breathing hard from fear, Sattler listens to Hammond's directions. "...straight ahead there's a metal staircase. Go for it..."

While Grant and the children climb higher, Sattler takes a wrong turning. But

Muldoon and Sattler know there's a Raptor out there somewhere!

Tim 'freezes' on the electrified fence!

Malcolm is able to get her back on course and she eventually arrives at a big metal box which contains the circuit breaker switches. "Now what?" she asks.

"You can't throw the main switch by hand, you have to pump up the primer handle to give you a charge," explains Hammond.

"I see it..."

Now, Grant and the children are swinging over the top of the fence.

In the shed, a small indicator light chings from 'Discharged' to 'Charged'. "Ready," shouts Sattler.

"There's a green button that says, 'Push to Close'. Push it," instructs Hammond. Sattler pushes the button.

A warning light flashes next to Grant's hand. He lets go of the fence and drops to the ground. He yells at the children, "Get off the fence. *Now!!*"

Sattler watches twelve indicator lights flash on. "The buttons turn on the individual Park systems," says Hammond. "Hit them all."

She begins to punch the buttons one by one. The last one is labelled 'Perimeter Fences'.

Lex drops off the fence, but Tim is still near the top. "Come on, Tim!" yells Grant, looking up at the warning light which is flashing faster now. "*Move!*"

But Tim freezes, unable to move.

Sattler is six buttons away from the last.

Grant and Lex both scream at Tim. "I'll catch you," yells Grant. "Just let go!"

"I'm okay, I'm going again," says Tim.

"No! No! No! It's too late. Let go! Let go!"

Sattler punches the last button.

"I can make it..." says Tim, as the fence comes alive with a *'Pow!'*, throwing the boy to the ground.

Grant races over to him. "He's not breathing."

Sattler watches the floor lights coming on, spreading towards her in rows. Then, behind the control panel, she sees...*a Raptor!*

It lashes out at her, but its feet are caught in the maze of pipes. Sattler falls backwards, then screams as a dead arm falls onto her shoulder. It belongs to Arnold, or what's left of him.

She runs back towards the door, slamming it behind her and hearing the Raptor snarling from the top of the stairs.

In the jungle, a snake slithers past what looks like the iris of a large flower. Then it blinks - it is a Raptor's eye.

Muldoon sees it, raises his gun and gives a half smile as his finger tenses on the trigger. "Gotcha!"

But the smile quickly disappears as his eyes flick to the side - which is where the attack comes from.

A second Raptor roars out of the foliage. The gun fires wildly as a claw rips through Muldoon's mid-section. He screams as the animal goes to work...all teeth and claws.

Grant has performed CPR on Tim and the boy is okay again, except for burnt hands, frizzled hair and near exhaustion!

They reach the deserted Visitors' Centre. Grant sits Tim in a chair in the restaurant, then goes off to find the others.

Lex gets Tim something to eat. But before he can take a mouthful, she freezes. "Something's here."

A Raptor creeps through the lobby.

"Can you run?"

"I don't think so," says Tim.

She loops an arm around him and hauls him into the kitchen. Quietly, she closes the door. But there's no lock on it...

The Raptor's head appears in the window, its breath steaming up the glass. It sniffs at the bottom of the door, then stands again, tilting its head curiously. It bumps the handle with its snout, reaches out a claw and opens the door!

Another Raptor is close behind. They enter the kitchen, snarling and bumping into each other. Each takes a separate aisle while Lex and Tim crawl away along a third.

Tim brushes against some hanging utensils and both Raptors turn, sniffing in his direction. One jumps onto the counter, knocking pots and pans onto the floor.

Then they are distracted by Lex, tapping a spoon on the floor at the other end of the aisle. The Raptor on the counter jumps down to investigate.

Lex slides open the door of a steel cabinet and crawls inside. She tries to close the door, but it is stuck.

One Raptor sees Lex's reflection in the shiny steel, the other sees Tim dragging himself towards a walk-in freezer. Both go into a pre-attack crouch - one towards each of the children.

The first one pounces and thuds into the reflection. It has chosen the wrong image and falls semi-conscious to the floor.

The other attacks Tim, who pulls open the door of the freezer and darts inside, slipping over on the slick floor. The Raptor slides in after him and falls over too.

Tim drags himself to his feet and makes for the door as the animal lunges at him with its mouth wide open.

Tim rushes out and Lex slams the door, catching the Raptor's head for a moment before it retreats. Tim jams the locking-pin into the handle, trapping the dinosaur in the freezer.

As the other Raptor staggers to its feet, Lex throws an arm around Tim and pulls him towards the restaurant. Then they bump into a dark shape ahead of them - *it's Grant and Sattler!*

Grant carries a rifle. "Let's go."

"We can call for help..." says Lex.

"...As soon as we re-boot the system," agrees Sattler, as they both head for the main console in the control room.

Grant sits Tim on a chair, then returns to the door. "Hey! The latch panel doesn't..."

Both children scream as something hits the door from the outside. Sattler races across to help Grant as a Raptor tries to force its way inside.

"The door lock," yells Grant. "Boot up the door locks!"

"You can't hold the door by yourself," cries Sattler.

Lex stares at the screen. Her fingers fly over the keyboard and the computer begins to respond to her commands. She touches a 'Door Integrity' box on the screen. The door latch panel buzzes, Sattler and Grant push harder and the door snicks shut...

The phone rings. Hammond grabs it. "...Grant!"

"We've got the phones back on. Call the mainland," says Grant's voice. "Have them send a helicopter..." But his sentence is cut short. There is a scream, followed by three gunshots.

"Grant! Grant!" cries Hammond into the 'phone. But there is no reply.

The Raptors move in!

Grant's rifle and spent shells lay on the floor and there are three impact patterns in the window. Suddenly the window shatters and a Raptor explodes into the control room.

Grant, Sattler and the children are climbing a ladder into the ceiling crawl space.

The curious Raptor tilts its head at the swaying ceiling, then leaps at it, smashing its head through one of the panels.

The humans are terrified, but keep moving, as the Raptor drops again. Then it erupts through another panel right in front of them, its teeth only inches from Dr Sattler.

"Get in the air duct!" commands Grant.

As they move towards the duct, the Raptor bursts through again, lifting the screaming Lex on top of its head. Grant smashes his boot into the head. The mouth snaps at him and catches his foot. Then it falls, ripping the sole from Grant's boot.

As the Raptor pounces again, Grant grabs Lex by the collar and pulls her back from the gaping hole.

They make their way through the duct, until they see light filtering through a grating. They are above the skeletons in the lobby. "Down through here," says Grant, climbing down onto a scaffold platform. "It's okay, come on."

"We're gonna make it... We're..." Sattler is cut short by the sudden shriek of claw on metal, as the Raptor lands on the scaffolding.

"Go down, down, down. Go! Go!" yells Grant, as the dinosaur springs onto the neck of the Sauropod skeleton.

An anchor bolt in the ceiling rips free and the skeleton collapses. Humans and Raptor fall to the ground in a cascade of bones. The Raptor is winded and on its back.

Grant and Sattler grab the children,

Sattler clings on!

ready to run. But they stop dead in their tracks - another Raptor stands in the doorway, already into its pre-attack crouch.

Suddenly there is a hideous ripping noise, and a huge shadow falls over the lobby. A massive head descends and a set of six foot jaws clamp on one of the Raptors which howls in agony.

The humans look in astonishment as the Raptor is lifted twenty feet into the air, *in the mouth of a Tyrannosaurus Rex!*

The Rex stands in front of the massive hole it has ripped in the wall. It shakes its head once, breaking the neck of the Raptor which falls dead to the floor.

A Jeep screeches to a halt outside. Hammond and Malcolm are inside.

The second Raptor leaps at the side of the Rex, tearing the flesh with its six inch razor-claws. As the humans skirt the battle and make a dash for the door, the Rex bellows in agony. Then it strikes the Raptor in the back and rips the body in half.

From the Jeep, the group see the Rex's tail lashing out and smashing the Tryrannosaur skeleton, in an explosion of bones.

"By the way," says Grant. "After careful consideration, I've decided *not* to endorse Jurassic Park."

"After careful consideration, so have I," replies Hammond, hitting the gas pedal.

The Jeep speeds towards the helicopter pad...

THE
DINOSAURS

Besides a cast of brilliant actors and actresses, *Jurassic Park* also features stars of a different magnitude - the dinosaurs in the Park!

The inhabitants of John Hammond's incredible theme park were made by a supremely talented creative team who have achieved a level of realism and technical innovation never before captured on film.

The group - among the first production elements recruited by Steven Spielberg and producer Kathleen Kennedy - includes the highly acclaimed Stan Winston (live action dinosaurs), Dennis Muren (full motion dinosaurs), Phil Tippett (dinosaur supervisor) and Michael Lantieri (special dinosaur effects). Added to this talented bunch were certain special visual effects created by the renowned Industrial Light & Magic company.

The dinosaurs were brought to life in different ways. Some were computer generated and some were full-scale props.

The main objective was to be totally convincing to the cinema-goer.

IN THE PARK

DINO-FAX

'Tyrannosaurus Rex' translates as 'Tyrant Lizard King'.

T-Rex was capable of devouring over a ton of food in a single meal!

T-Rex skeletons have been found in Alberta, Canada and Montana, USA.

TYRANNOSAURUS REX

Tyrannosaurus Rex is the most famous of all dinosaurs and is believed to be among the most ferocious of the carnivores of the late Cretaceous period.

Between 18 and 25 feet tall and up to 40 feet in length, Tyrannosaurus has huge powerful jaws which can swallow man-sized animals whole.

Tyrannosaurus Rex causes mayhem and terror whenever and wherever it appears in *Jurassic Park*.

The terrifying Tyrannosaurus Rex - just look at those teeth and those beady, yellow eyes!

TRICERATOPS

Sattler and Grant examine the sick
Triceratops

A heavy lumbering animal with strong, stumpy legs, Triceratops is built low to the ground and is about the size of an elephant. It has a massive head from which three horns protude - the longest from the middle of the forehead.

Although ferocious looking, Triceratops is really quite docile.

In *Jurassic Park*, Dr Sattler, Dr Grant and Tim discover that a sick Triceratops has been swallowing poisonous berries.

DINO-FAX

'Triceratops' translates as 'three horned face', and was named by the famous Othniel Marsh in 1889.

Triceratops skeletons have been discovered in the USA and western Canada.

Triceratops fed by grazing on grasses and other plant life.

Gallimimus has a long neck and a short, flattish snout

About the size of an antelope, Gallimimus is a herd animal. They are fast runners, but not always fast enough to outpace the T-Rex who considers them a truly tasty treat!

In *Jurassic Park*, a whole herd of Gallimimus features in a spectacular stampede in which they are chased by a hungry Rex.

DINO-FAX

The word 'Gallimimus' means 'hen mimic'.

Gallimimus bones have been found in southern Mongolia.

It is believed that Gallimimus found its food by scratching in the earth.

GALLIMIMUS

A Raptor in the kitchen!

VELOCIRAPTOR

The 'Raptors' are definitely the scariest creatures in *Jurassic Park*, and have been called 'the most vicious dinosaurs that ever lived'.

They are as intelligent as chimpanzees and can even solve problems. In the movie we learn how they 'test' the electrified fence.

Standing around six feet tall, the Raptors have a six inch retractable razor-sharp claw on each foot. These claws are used to devastating effect and can kill a man with a single swipe. The Raptor is a fast mover too - "Cheetah speed - 50-60 mph," confirms Robert Muldoon in the movie.

It does seem that the Velociraptors hunt and kill for sport, often leading their prey into an ambush situation.

A vicious Raptor stalks its prey

DINO-FAX

'Velociraptor' translates as 'fast thief'.

A Velociraptor skeleton was discovered in 1971, together with that of a Protoceratops. It is thought that the two creatures died in combat.

The Dilophosaurus which stalks Dennis Nedry

You could be forgiven for thinking that the Dilophosaurus is a friendly, playful creature. That's what it wants you to think as it hoots and scoots around you!

Once it has lured its victim into a false sense of security, the Dilophosaurus snaps its head back and spits globs of venom that blinds and paralyses its unsuspecting prey.

In *Jurassic Park*, computer programmer Dennis Nedry becomes a classic Dilophosaurus victim.

The animal stands around four feet tall with two curious fins on its head. It is spotted like an owl and has a brilliantly coloured crest in *Jurassic Park* which fans out when the Dilophosaurus is about to strike.

DILOPHOSAURUS

DINO-FAX

The word 'Dilophosaurus' means 'two ridged reptile'.

Dilophosaurus bones have been excavated in Arizona.

Dilophosaurus is listed among the oldest of carnivores.

The Dilophosaurus crest

Known as the tallest of the dinosaurs, the Brachiosaurus stands at over 50 feet. It has a long neck and a long tail for balance.

A single Brachiosaurus weighs in at around 30 tons - that's more than an entire herd of present day elephants!

They are friendly animals wearing a simple expression on their tiny faces. Despite their great size, they seem almost harmless, being only interested in eating vegetation.

This is shown in the movie when Grant, Lex and Tim are awoken by a Brachiosaurus feeding on branches right next to them. The animal even allows Grant to pull down its lip so he can observe the jaws in action!

Brachiosaurus, the gentle giant of Jurassic Park, feeds right next to Grant, Lex and Tim

DINO-FAX

Brachiosaurus is also known as Brontosaurus.

The word 'Brachiosaurus' means 'arm reptile'.

Brachiosaurus skeletons have been found in Colorado and Tanzania.

BRACHIOSAURUS

SAM NEILL
as
DR ALAN GRANT

Sam Neill plays renowned paleontologist Dr Alan Grant - the dinosaur expert who gets a lot more than he bargained for when he visits Jurassic Park.

Grant is intensely focused on his work and is accustomed to roughing it on dinosaur digs around the world. He is romantically involved with his colleague, Dr Ellie Sattler. He doesn't particularly like children - until his terrifying adventure with Lex and Tim.

Sam Neill was born in Northern Ireland, but raised in New Zealand. He graduated from the University of Canterbury before beginning his acting career with the Amamus Theatre Group. Later he combined acting and directing with the New Zealand Film Unit.

Among Neill's earliest film roles, and the one that gained him international recognition, was that of Harry Beecham in the Australian hit, *My Brilliant Career*, in which he played opposite Judy Davis.

Neill went on to appear in other movies, including the exciting thriller, *Dead Calm*, *Memoirs of an Invisible Man*, *The Hunt for Red October* and *A Cry In The Dark*, for which he won the Australian Film Institute's 'Best Actor' Award.

Neill is well-known to TV viewers for his performance in the thriller series, *Reilly, Ace of Spies*. His portrayal of Sidney Reilly, 'the greatest spy the world has ever known', earned him a 'Best Actor' Award in Britain and a Golden Globe nomination in the USA.

Among Neill's other memorable small screen successes are, *The Sinking of the Rainbow Warrior*, *Hostage*, *Fever*, *Amerika*, and the 1986 mini-series *Kane and Abel*.

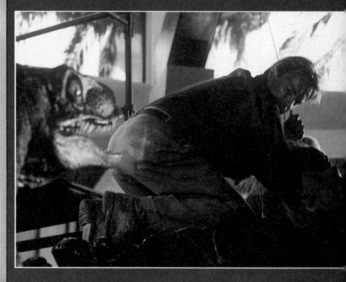

Main picture: Sam Neill as Dr Alan Grant
Below: Alan Grant questions John Hammond, while Dr Ellie Sattler looks on
Right: Grant has a close encounter with a raptor!

LAURA DERN

Paleobotanist Dr Ellie Sattler works alongside Dr Alan Grant and is invited to accompany him as one of the first people to visit Jurassic Park.

In her late-20s, Ellie is very ambitious and a little impatient. She is in love with Alan and one day hopes they will marry and have children.

Laura Dern comes from a famous acting background. Her father is Bruce Dern, her mother Diane Ladd.

Dern made her movie debut at the tender age of seven, when director Martin Scorsese included her as an extra in the film *Alice Doesn't Live Here Anymore*, in which her mother was appearing.

Four years later, the young Miss Dern made her professional screen debut in *Foxes*, an anti-drugs drama starring Jodie Foster. She later studied drama at the Lee Strasberg Institute in America and The Royal Academy Of Dramatic Art in London.

In 1985, Dern received the Los Angeles Film Critics Award for her portrayal of an emotional teenager in *Smooth Talk*. She has appeared in a number of other notable films including *Teachers, Mask, Blue Velvet, Wild at Heart* and *Rambling Rose*, for which she received Oscar and Golden Globe 'Best Actress' nominations.

Main picture: Dr Ellie Sattler looks back in terror as she is persued by a vicious Velociraptor!
Left: More tension for Ellie Sattler, played by Laura Dern.
Right: Ellie Sattler with Alan Grant

Sir Richard Attenborough portrays the billionaire entrepreneur/showman John Hammond - the man who transforms his dreams of Jurassic Park into a frightening reality.

Hammond is a forceful, energetic and sprightly seventy-something. He has a slight limp, although many suspect that he carries a walking cane only for effect!

As an actor and director, Richard Attenborough is among the giants of cinema.

When he was just 17 years old, Attenborough began his acting career in film with an auspicious start. It was in the 1942 classic wartime drama, *In Which We Serve*, written by Noel Coward and co-directed by Coward and David Lean. Attenborough's performance, as a young sailor who deserts his post, won him many admirers - and he never looked back.

A string of films followed with Attenborough generally playing baby-faced juveniles throughout the late-40s, (including a chilling performance as Pinkie in the movie adaptation of Graham Greene's 'Brighton Rock', before landing adult roles in the '50s.

In 1960, he turned to production with *The Angry Silence*, followed in 1964 by *Seance on a Wet Afternoon*, both of which met with huge critical acclaim.

Attenborough has acted in blockbusters such as *The Great Escape* and *Doctor Dolittle*, as well as giving a finely tuned performance as the murderer, Reginald Christie, in *Ten Rillington Place*.

Attenborough made his directing debut in 1969, with *Oh! What a Lovely War*. Next came *Young Winston*, *A Bridge Too Far*, *Magic* and the multi-Oscar winning *Gandhi*, starring Ben Kingsley as the Indian advocate who became a martyr.

The glitzy showbiz drama, *A Chorus Line*, was followed by *Cry Freedom* and more recently, *Chaplin*, the biography of cinema's most famous comedian.

Main picture: Richard Attenborough as John Hammond - the man who built Jurassic Park
Above: Hammond presides over lunch in the Jurassic Park restaurant
Below: "Welcome to Jurassic Park," says John Hammond

RICHARD ATTENBOROUGH

as

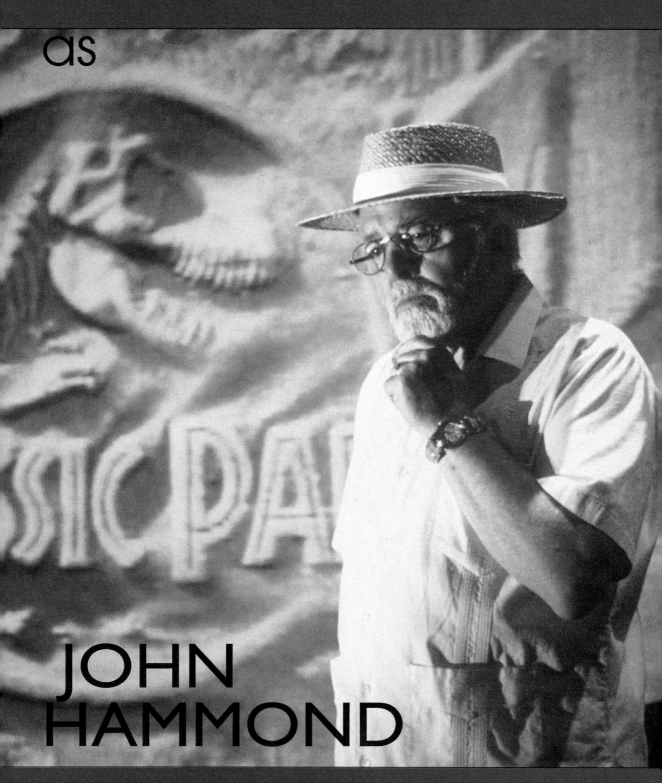

JOHN HAMMOND

JEFF GOLDBLUM

as

DR IAN MALCOLM

Above: Malcolm gets to know Ellie Sattler

Left: Jeff Goldblum plays Dr Ian Malcolm - the hip
Chaotician who predicts disaster for Jurassic Park

Jeff Goldblum portrays the mathematician, Dr Ian Malcolm, who doubts the propriety of Jurassic Park from the outset.

He believes that the interaction of systems in Jurassic Park and the unknown depths of bioengineering are far too complex - and therefore bound to fail.

Malcolm warns John Hammond against tampering with nature and, at every opportunity, uses 'Chaos Theory' to back up his predictions.

A hip character, Malcolm dresses in black, wearing sunglasses and snakeskin boots.

Jeff Goldblum has an impressive list of movie credits to his name. These include *Nashville*, *Invasion of the Body Snatchers*, *The Right Stuff*, *The Big Chill*, *Silverado*, *The Tall Guy*, *Mister Frost*, - as well as the remarkably gruesome, *The Fly*, in which he transmutes into the insect of the title.

JOSEPH MAZZELLO
as TIM

Tim and Lex

Tim is in big trouble

John Hammond's nine-year-old grandson Tim, played by Joseph Mazzello, is a real dinosaur fan. He has read many books on the subject, including one written by his hero, Dr Alan Grant, and can put a name to nearly all the pre-historic animals.

Tim is thrilled to be visiting Jurassic Park - but will he still love dinosaurs when the visit comes to an end?

Young Joseph Mazzello made his movie debut when he was just five in a TV film called *Unspeakable Acts*. Since then, he's appeared in *Radio Flyer*, *Presumed Innocent*, *Jersey Girls* and the TV movie, *Desperate Choices: Save My Child*.

ARIANA RICHARDS

as LEX

Lex can hardly believe her eyes as the T-rex approaches

Lex, portrayed by Ariana Richards, is the twelve - year-old granddaughter of John Hammond and elder sister of Tim.

Lex is something of a tomboy and sees herself as a pretty good computer hacker. Indeed, her computer skills prove more than useful in the battle with the Raptors!

Having made her first TV commercial at the age of seven, Ariana is already something of a screen veteran. In 1991, she won the Youth In Film Award for 'Best Young Actress' starring in a TV movie for her role in *Switched At Birth*. She repeated that success in 1992 for her role in *Locked Up*.

Ariana's other TV roles have included appearances in *The Golden Girls, Empty Nest, My Sister Sam* and the series, *Island Son*, with Richard Chamberlain.

Ariana has appeared in a number of feature films including *Disaster In Time, Tremors, Spaced Invaders, Prancer, Into The Homeland* and *I'm Gonna Git You, Sucka*.

BOB PECK as

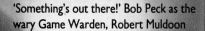

'Something's out there!' Bob Peck as the wary Game Warden, Robert Muldoon

Inset: Muldoon and Sattler discover the injured Malcolm

Robert Muldoon is Jurassic Park's Chief Game Warden. He is a powerful, authoritative figure who has spent most of his life working with wild animals.

But even such an experienced hunter had to adopt new skills when dealing with dinosaurs.

Muldoon is killed when he attempts to outsmart a Velociraptor.

Muldoon is portrayed by British actor, Bob Peck, who starred in the BBC's acclaimed 1986 thriller, *Edge of Darkness*.

ROBERT MULDOON

WAYNE KNIGHT
as DENNIS NEDRY

Dennis Nedry (Wayne Knight) wonders what the Dilophosaurus will do next!

Inset: Nedry is a big man, with a big appetite for food and money!

Dennis Nedry is a computer genius employed by John Hammond to program all the Jurassic Park computer systems.

A big guy with a constant grin, Nedry is fond of sweets and video games.

Unfortunately, he also has money worries which lead him to sabotage the system while attempting to smuggle dinosaur embryos from Isla Nublar.

Nedry meets with a particularly sticky end when he tangles with the spitting Dilophosaurus.

Dennis Nedry is brilliantly portrayed by Wayne Knight.

Steven Spielberg - the man with the 'golden touch'

STEVEN SPIELBERG

MASTER OF THE MOVIES

With a reputation as one of the world's most respected and successful talents, Steven Spielberg has directed and/or produced six of the top twenty films of all time.

E.T. The Extra-Terrestrial directed by Spielberg and produced by Kathleen Kennedy, is still the biggest grossing film in the history of motion pictures.

At the 1987 Academy Award ceremonies, his consisent excellence in film-making was rewarded with the prestigious Irving G. Thalberg Award. For his direction on *The Color Purple*, Spielberg earned the coveted Directors Guild of America Award in 1986. The film also received eleven Academy Award nominations.

For his work on the following five films, Spielberg has been nominated by the DGA: *Empire of the Sun*, *Jaws*, *Close Encounters of the Third Kind*, *Raiders of the Lost Ark* and *E.T. The Extra-Terrestrial*. For the latter three, he was also nominated by the Academy of Motion Picture Arts and Sciences.

Sugarland Express marked Spielberg's feature directing debut. The two films that followed, *Jaws* and *Close Encounters of the Third Kind*, were phenomenal successes.

Following *1941*, his World War II comedy, Spielberg teamed with longtime friend George Lucas to make *Raiders of the Lost Ark*, which he directed and Lucas executive produced. *Poltergeist* followed in 1982 which he co-wrote and co-produced while concurrently directing *E.T.*

Spielberg collaborated again with George Lucas on *Indiana Jones and the Temple of Doom* and five years later on *Indiana Jones and the Last Crusade*. His other directing credits include a segment of *Twilight Zone - The Movie*, *Always* and *Hook*.

In 1984, Spielberg formed Amblin Entertainment, his own production company. He has since executive produced over a dozen films including *Gremlins*, *The Goonies*, *Back to the Future*, as well as *Back to the Future II and III*, *An American Tail*, *Who Framed Roger Rabbit?* and *The Land Before Time*.

While working on post-production for *Jurassic Park*, Spielberg's latest project, *Schindler's List*, starring Liam Neeson and Ben Kingsley, began filming in Poland in March, 1993.

Amblin Television and Amblin Entertainment have been working in both network and syndicated series programs and television specials.

Amongst these has been 'Screen Works', a minimum of six two hour films for the Turner Television Network, produced by Amblin and Michael Brandman Productions. Other projects include: the Emmy Award winning syndicated series *Tiny Toon Adventures*, the recent ABC-TV movie *Class of '61*, the animated CBS-TV series programs *Back to the Future* and *Fievel's American Tails*, specials based on *Back to the Future* and *Who Framed Roger Rabbit?* and the NBC-TV anthology series *Amazing Stores*.

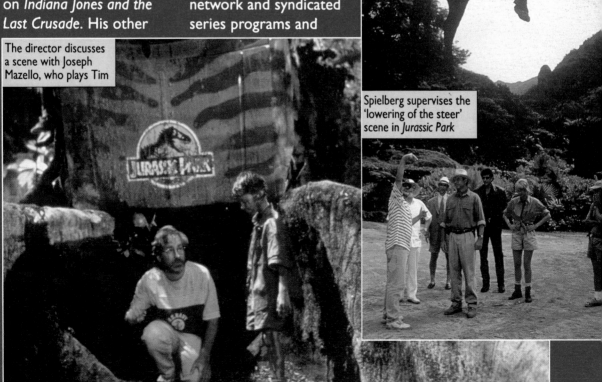

The director discusses a scene with Joseph Mazello, who plays Tim

Spielberg supervises the 'lowering of the steer' scene in *Jurassic Park*

STEVEN SPIELBERG FILMOGRAPHY

YEAR	FILM	CREDIT	STUDIO
	AMBLIN (35mm short)	Director, Writer	
1973	DUEL (TV-Released Theatrically in Europe)	Director	Universal
1974	SUGARLAND EXPRESS	Director, Story by	Universal
1975	JAWS	Director	Universal
1977	CLOSE ENCOUNTERS OF THE THIRD KIND	Director, Writer	Columbia
1978	I WANNA HOLD YOUR HAND	*Executive Producer	Universal
1979	1941	Director	Universal
1980	USED CARS	*Executive Producer	Columbia
1981	RAIDERS OF THE LOST ARK	Director	Paramount
1982	POLTERGEIST	Producer, *Writer	MGM
1982	E.T. THE EXTRA-TERRESTRIAL	Director, *Producer	Universal
1983	TWILIGHT ZONE - THE MOVIE ('Kick the Can' Segment)	Director, *Producer	Warner Bros.
1984	INDIANA JONES AND THE TEMPLE OF DOOM	Director	Paramount
1984	GREMLINS	*Executive Producer	Warner Bros.
1985	FANDANGO	Amblin Entertainment Presentation	Warner Bros.
1985	THE GOONIES	*Executive Producer, Story by	Warner Bros.
1985	BACK TO THE FUTURE	*Executive Producer	Universal
1985	YOUNG SHERLOCK HOLMES	*Executive Producer	Paramount
1985	THE COLOR PURPLE	Director, *Producer	Warner Bros.
1986	THE MONEY PIT	*Executive Producer	Universal
1986	AN AMERICAN TAIL	*Executive Producer	Universal
1987	HARRY AND THE HENDERSONS	Universal Pictures/ Amblin Entertainment Production	Universal
1987	INNERSPACE	*Executive Producer	Warner Bros.
1987	EMPIRE OF THE SUN	Director, *Producer	Warner Bros.
1987	BATTERIES NOT INCLUDED	*Executive Producer	Universal
1988	WHO FRAMED ROGER RABBIT?	*Executive Producer	Disney
1988	THE LAND BEFORE TIME	*Executive Producer	Universal
1989	INDIANA JONES AND THE LAST CRUSADE	Director	Paramount
1989	DAD	*Executive Producer	Universal
1989	BACK TO THE FUTURE Part II	*Executive Producer	Universal
1989	ALWAYS	Director, *Producer	Universal
1990	DREAMS	Spielberg Presents	Warner Bros.
1990	JOE VERSUS THE VOLCANO	*Executive Producer	Warner Bros.
1990	GREMLINS II - THE NEW BATCH	*Executive Producer	Warner Bros.
1990	BACK TO THE FUTURE Part III	*Executive Producer	Universal
1990	ARACHNOPHOBIA	*Executive Producer	Hollywood Pictures
1991	CAPE FEAR	Amblin Ent. in Assoc.	Universal
1991	AN AMERICAN TAIL: FIEVEL GOES WEST	*Producer	Universal
1991	HOOK	Director	Tri-Star
1992	NOISES OFF	Amblin Ent. Presents	Touchstone
1993	A FAR OFF PLACE	Amblin Ent. Presents	Walt Disney
1993	JURASSIC PARK	Director	Universal

* Credit is shared with others

An Adventure

65 Million Years In The Making.

A STEVEN SPIELBERG FILM

JURASSIC PARK ™

UNIVERSAL PICTURES PRESENTS AN AMBLIN ENTERTAINMENT PRODUCTION SAM NEILL LAURA DERN JEFF GOLDBLUM
AND RICHARD ATTENBOROUGH "JURASSIC PARK" BOB PECK MARTIN FERRERO B.D. WONG SAMUEL L. JACKSON WAYNE KNIGHT
JOSEPH MAZZELLO ARIANA RICHARDS LIVE ACTION DINOSAURS STAN WINSTON FULL MOTION DINOSAURS BY DENNIS MUREN, A.S.C. DINOSAUR SUPERVISOR PHIL TIPPETT
SPECIAL DINOSAUR EFFECTS MICHAEL LANTIERI MUSIC JOHN WILLIAMS FILM EDITED MICHAEL KAHN, A.C.E. PRODUCTION DESIGNER RICK CARTER DIRECTOR OF PHOTOGRAPHY DEAN CUNDEY, A.S.C.
BASED ON THE NOVEL BY MICHAEL CRICHTON SCREENPLAY BY MICHAEL CRICHTON AND DAVID KOEPP PRODUCED BY KATHLEEN KENNEDY AND GERALD R. MOLEN A UNIVERSAL PICTURE
DIRECTED BY STEVEN SPIELBERG SPECIAL VISUAL EFFECTS BY INDUSTRIAL LIGHT & MAGIC

PG-13 PARENTS STRONGLY CAUTIONED
Some Material May Be Inappropriate for Children Under 13

DOLBY STEREO
IN SELECTED THEATRES

ORIGINAL SOUNDTRACK ON MCA CDs AND CASSETTES

READ THE BALLANTINE BOOK

AMBLIN ENTERTAINMENT

UNIVERSAL
AN MCA COMPANY

45